ANIMAL OPPOSITES

Dull and Colourful ANIMALS

Mark Carwardine

Wayland

Titles in this series
Noisy and Quiet Animals
Daytime and Night-time Animals
Quick and Slow Animals
Big and Small Animals
Sleepy and Busy Animals
Warm-Weather and Cold-Weather Animals
Prickly and Soft Animals

First published in 1988 by
Wayland (Publishers) Ltd.
61 Western Road, Hove
East Sussex BN3 1JD
England

© Copyright 1988 Ilex Publishers Limited

British Library Cataloguing in Publication Data

Carwardine, Mark
 Dull and Colourful animals.—
 (Animal opposites)
 1. Animals—Juvenile literature
 I. Title II. Series
 591 QL49

ISBN 1-85210-425-2

Created and produced by
Ilex Publishers Ltd
29–31 George Street
Oxford OX1 2AJ

Illustrations by Martin Camm
Courtesy of Bernard Thornton Artists

Typesetting by Optima Typographic, London
Printed in Spain by Gráficas Estella, S.A.

Cover illustration by Jim Channell
a mandrill and a moose

Contents

Moose	4
Torrent Duck	6
Bearded Seal	8
Mandrill	10
Potto	12
Flamingo	14
Sea Otter	16
Parrot (Scarlet Macaw)	18
Platypus	20
Kingfisher	22
Index	24
Glossary	24

Some words in this book are printed in **bold**; you can find out what they mean in the glossary on page 24.

The moose is a dull animal.

It likes to live near ponds and marshes and will paddle in the water for hours on end. This moose is hiding behind a tree.

Moose, or elk, as they are sometimes called, live in the northerly parts of North America, Europe and Asia. They are the largest deer in the world. Water plants are among their favourite foods. A hungry moose will eat over a thousand plants a day.

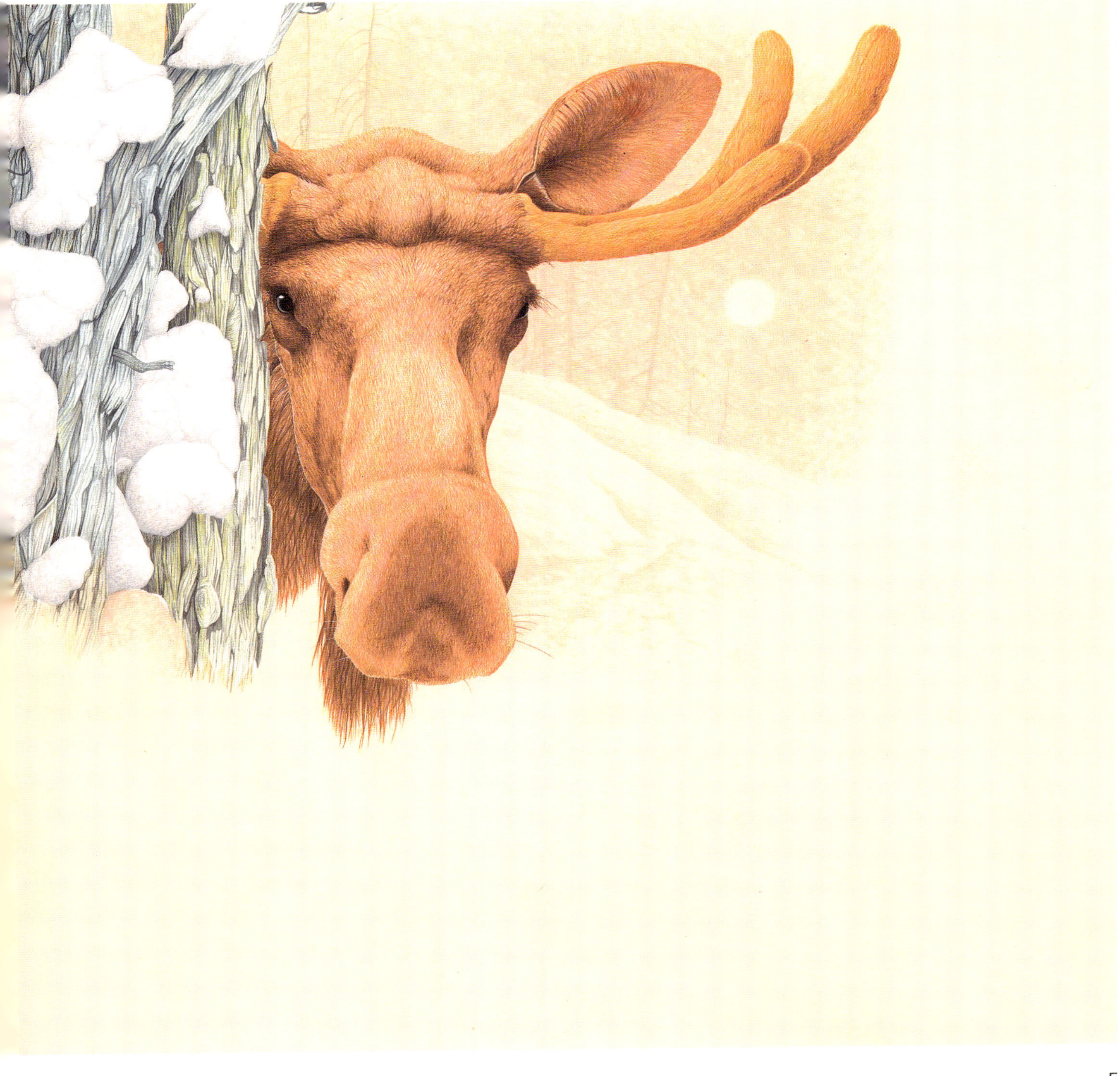

The torrent duck is a colourful animal.

It has a beautiful white head streaked with black.
This torrent duck is swimming in the swirling waters of a river.

Torrent ducks live in the rivers of the Andes Mountains, in South America. Their **webbed** feet are so enormous that their eggs have to be specially big for the unhatched chicks to fit inside.

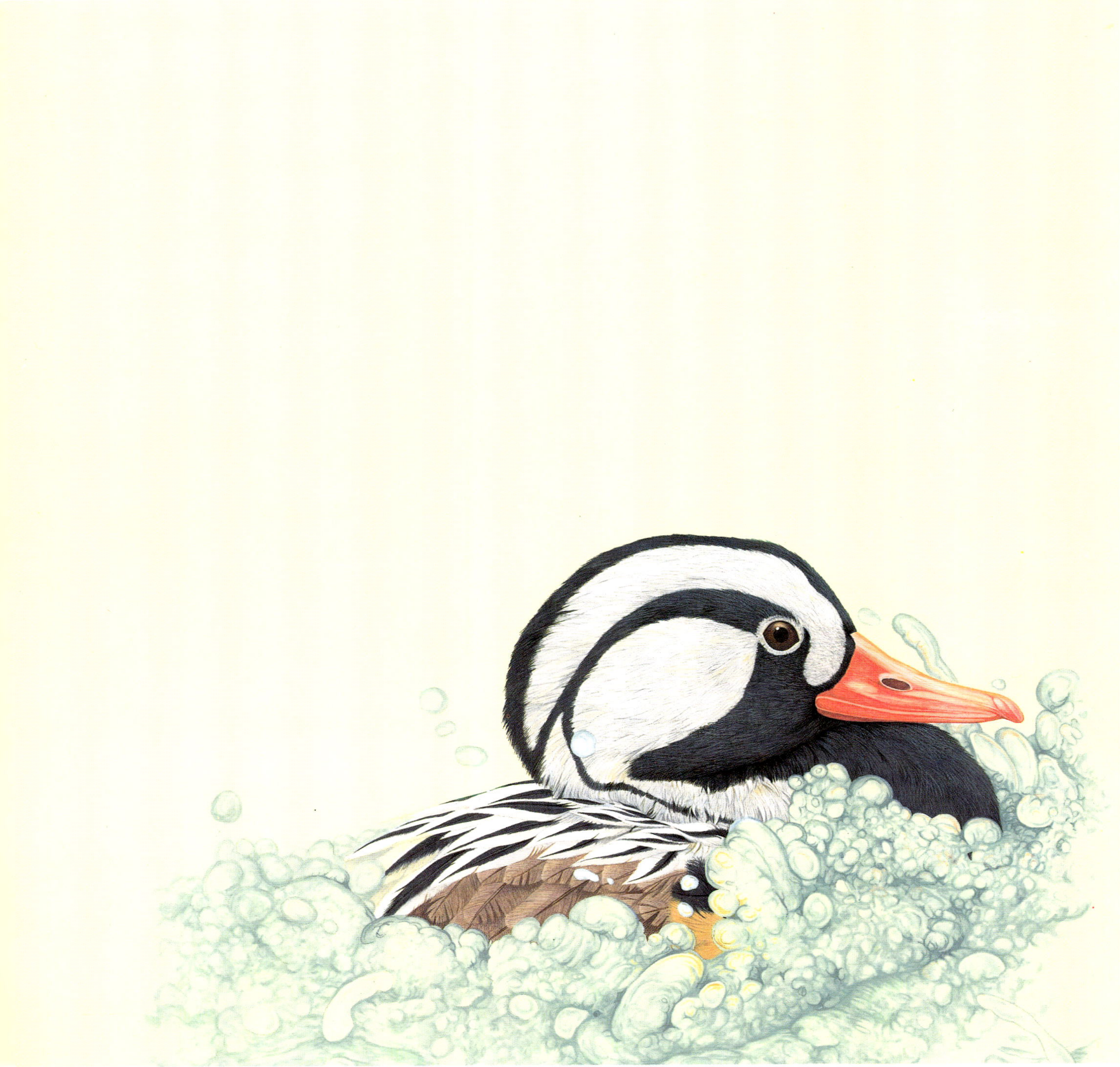

The bearded seal is a dull animal.

It is easily recognized by its long whiskers, which look rather like a beard or moustache. This bearded seal has just caught a fish.

Bearded seals live in the cold northern seas. They rarely swim very far out to sea, but prefer to stay in fairly shallow waters near the coast.

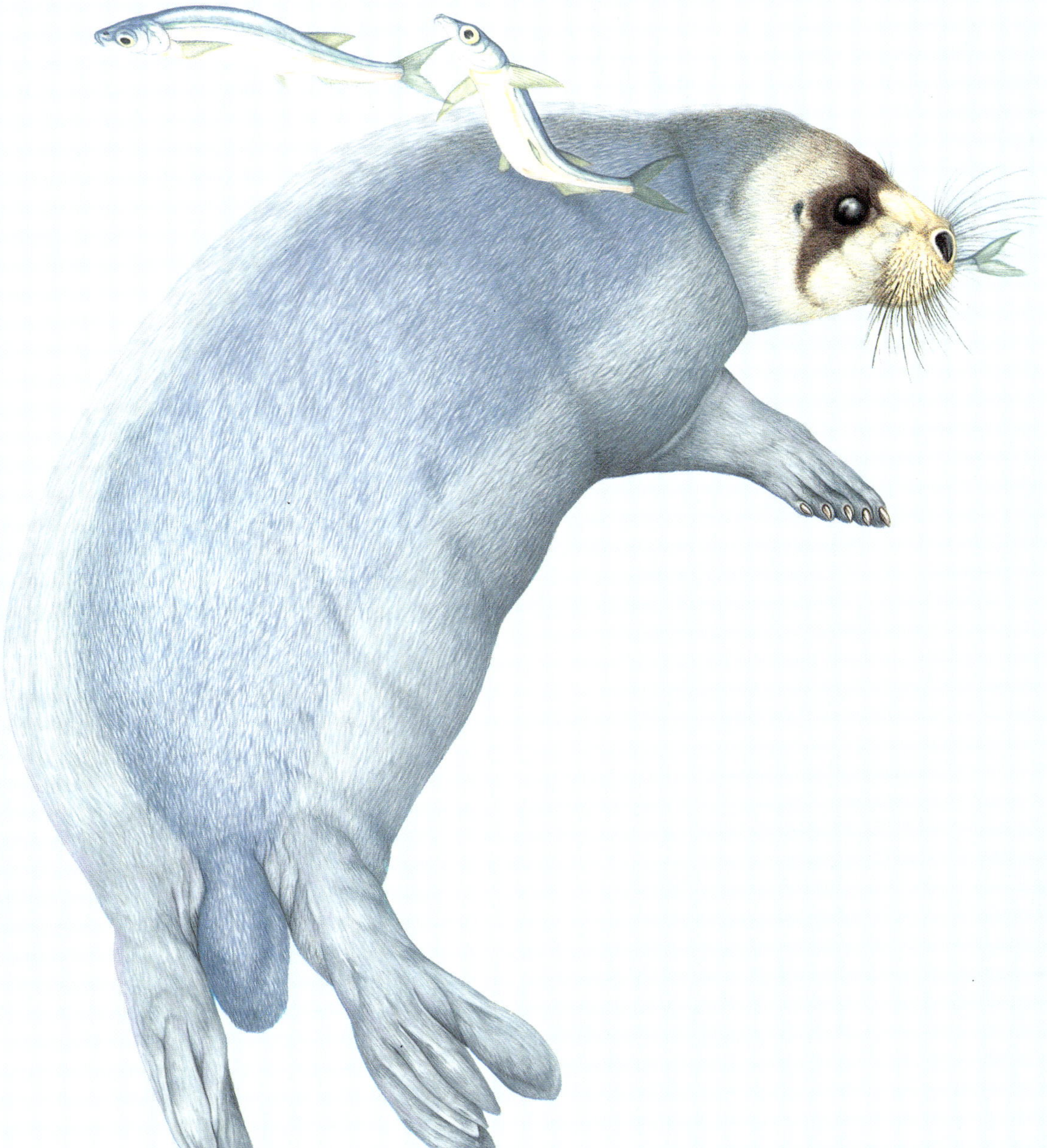

The mandrill is a colourful animal.

It has blue cheeks, a red nose and a bright yellow chin.
This mandrill is taking a rest in the shade.

When they get cross, mandrills often act like spoilt children; they moan and chatter to themselves, shake their heads and angrily slap the ground with their hands.

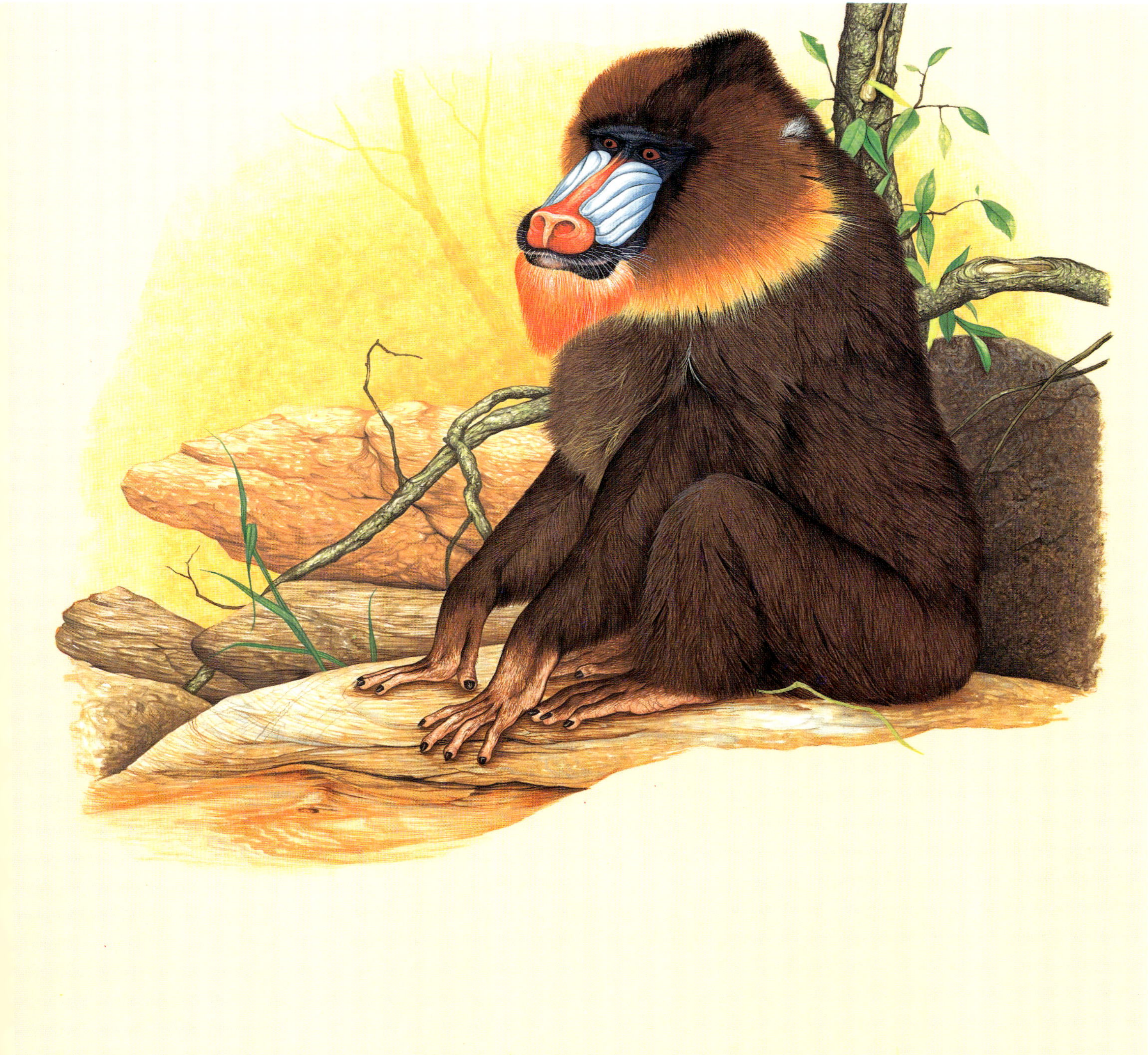

The potto is a dull animal.

It is very tough and can defend itself from most enemies by biting with its sharp teeth. This potto is hanging upside-down from a branch.

Although they are tough, pottos rarely fight in the wild. They prefer to stay still in the hope of not being seen. If they are in great danger, they simply let go of the branch they are on and fall to the ground.

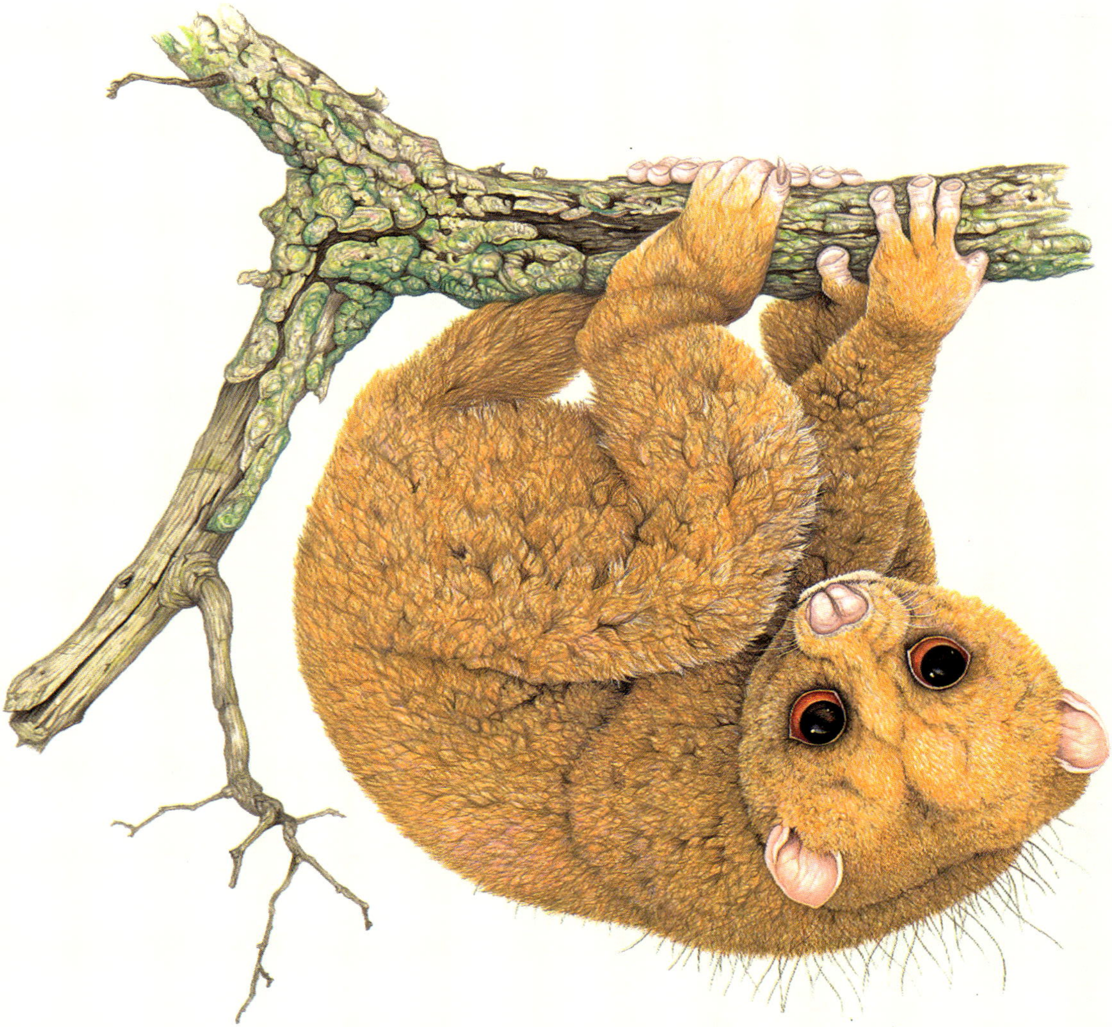

The flamingo is a colourful animal.

It has a bright pink body, pink legs and a pink and black **bill**.
This flamingo is feeding with its head upside-down in the water.

There are four kinds of flamingo, all fairly similar in appearance. Their bills are perfect for **filtering** out **minute** food particles from the water and mud.

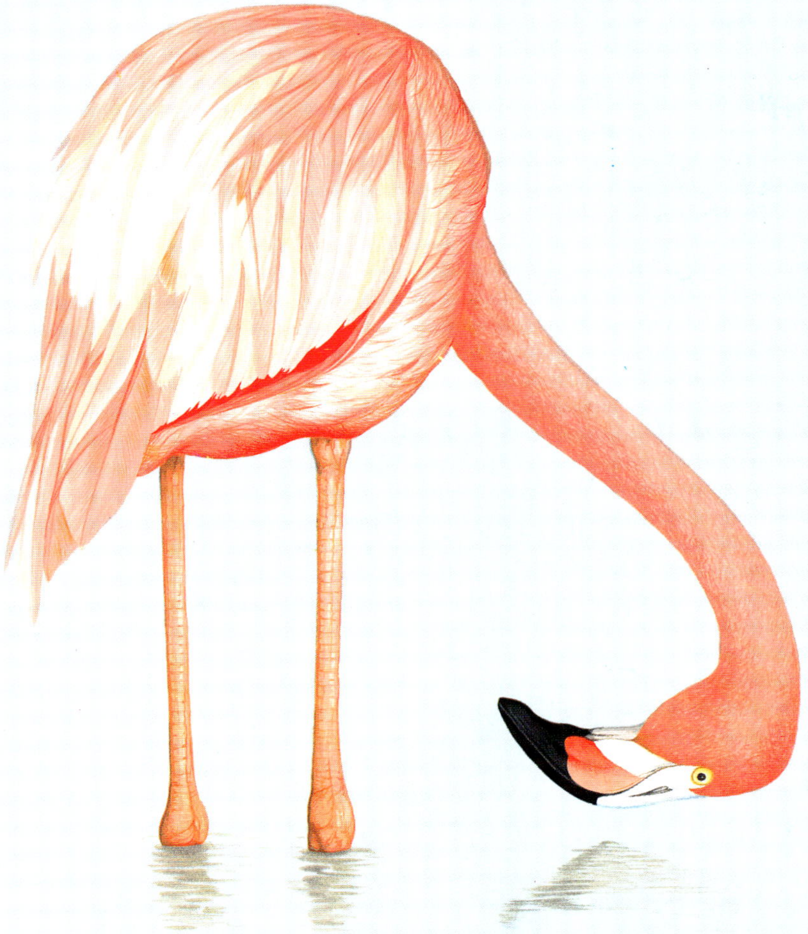

The sea otter is a dull animal.

It lives along the rocky coasts of western North America and eastern Russia.
This sea otter has tied itself to a giant seaweed to avoid drifting out to sea while it sleeps.

Sea otters spend most of their lives in the water, though never so far out that they might lose sight of the coast. Baby otters are even born in the water and ride on their mothers' chests for the first few weeks of their lives.

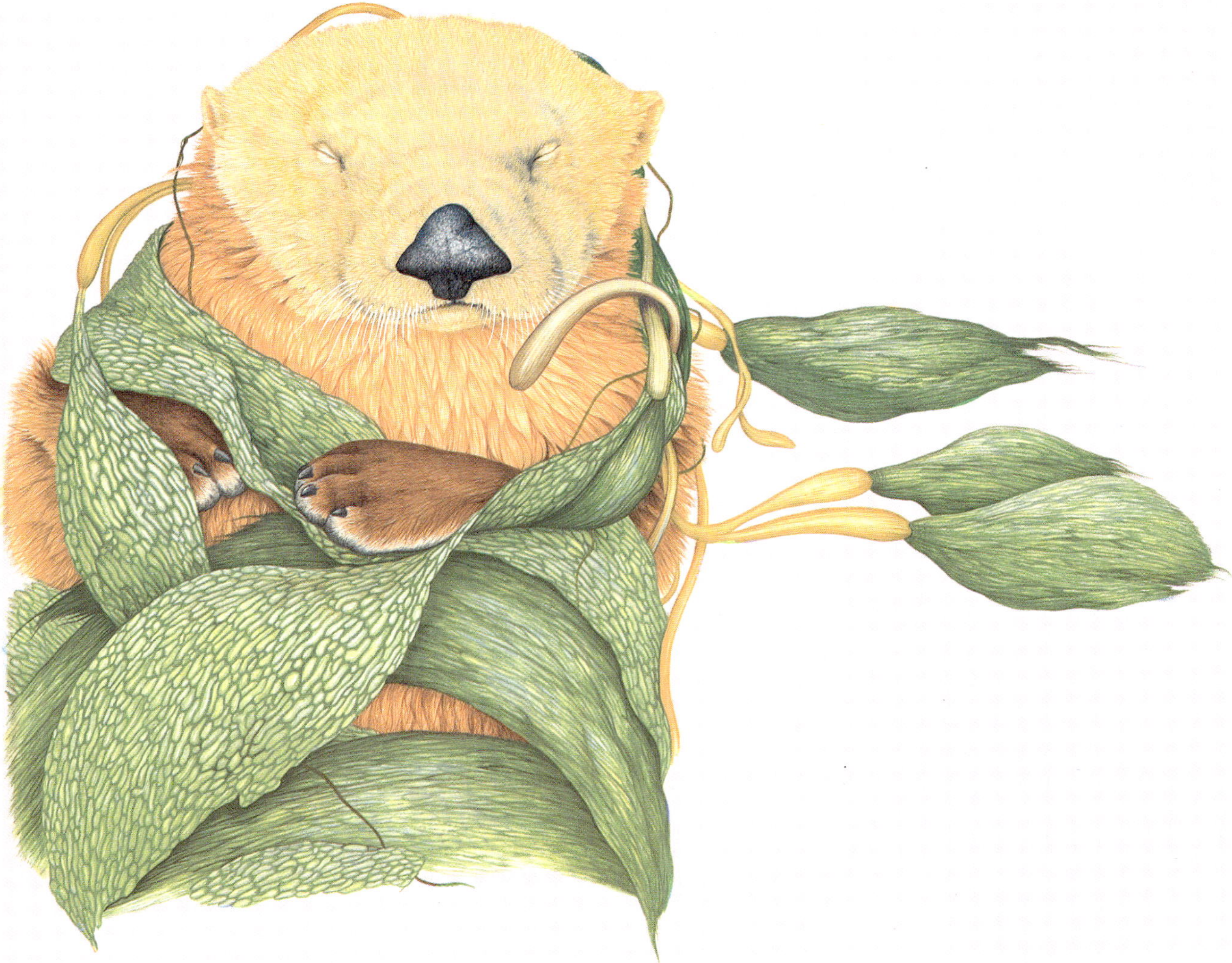

The macaw is a colourful animal.

It is one of the most brilliantly coloured of all birds.
This macaw has its nest in a hole in a tree.

Macaws are members of the parrot family, found in the jungles of Central and South America. Their strong beaks are used in climbing, to grasp higher branches while moving their feet forward. They are also adapted for cracking open tough nuts.

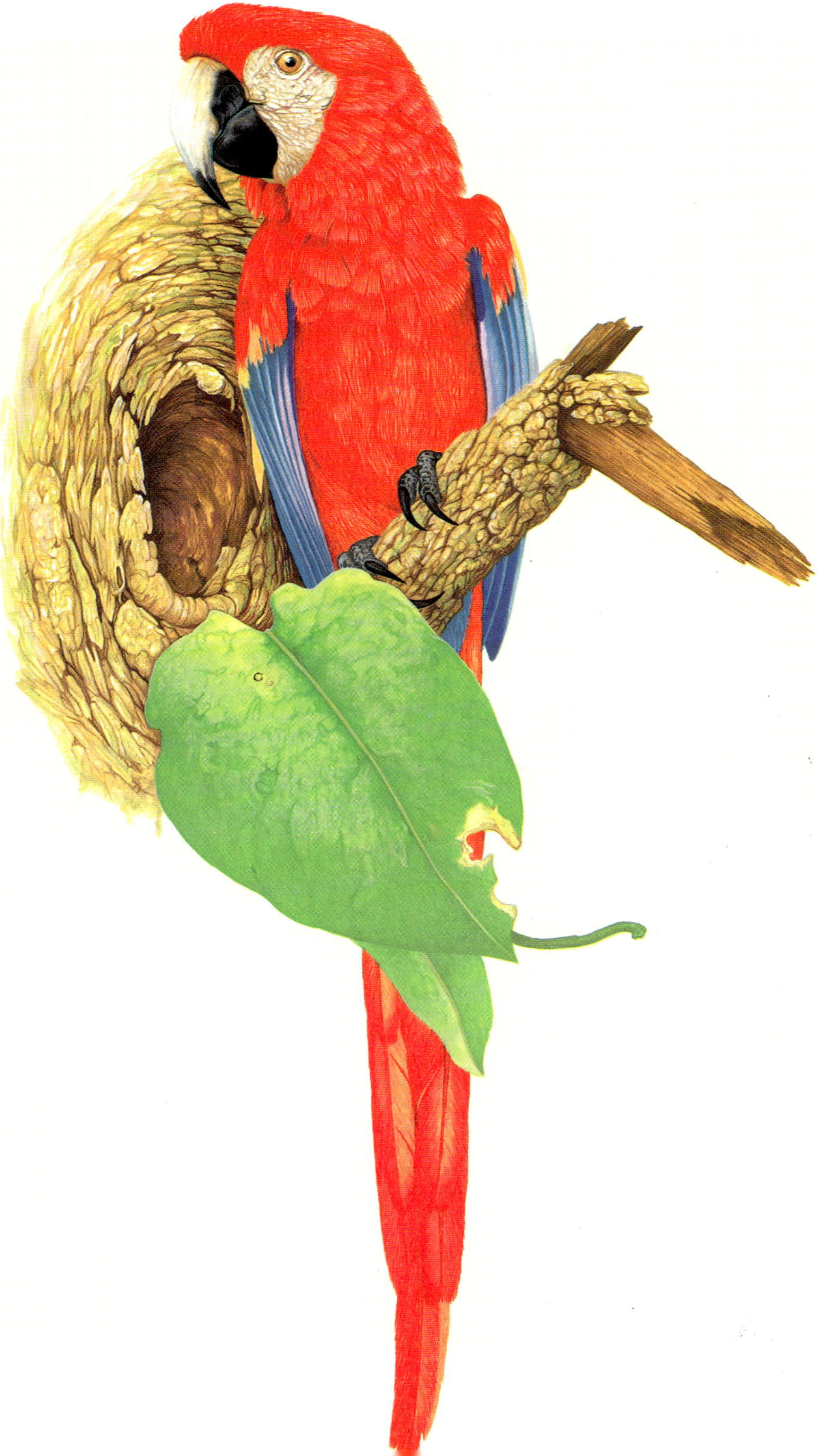

The duck-billed platypus is a dull animal.

It is a strange-looking creature, with webbed feet and a bill like a duck.
This platypus is scooping up insects and other food from the bottom of a lake.

Found in eastern Australia and Tasmania, the duck-billed platypus always closes its eyes and ears when it is diving underwater.
It hunts using its **sensitive** bill, or snout.

21

The kingfisher is a colourful animal.

It has a brilliant blue-green back and orange-chestnut front.
This kingfisher has just caught a small fish.

The European kingfisher catches fish by diving, either from a perch or after hovering above the water. The fish are always swallowed head-first and, if they have spines, are beaten to death first to make sure they are safe to swallow.

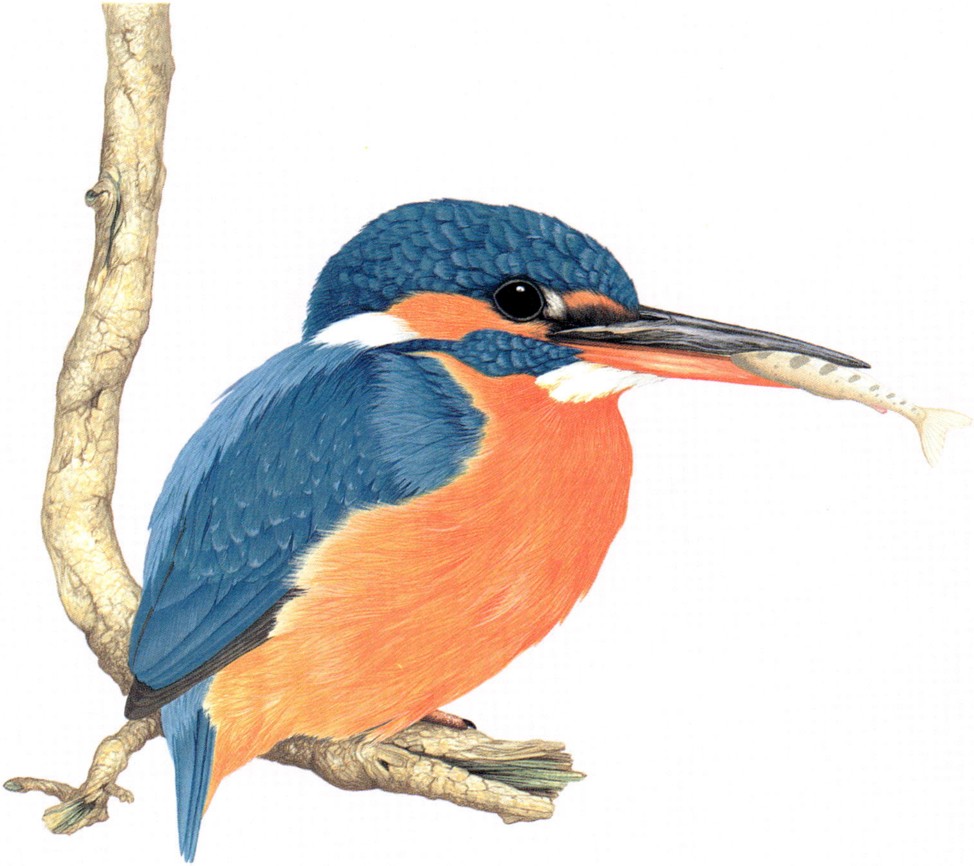

Index

Andes 6
Asia 4
Australia 20
Duck 6
Europe 4
Flamingo 14
Jungle 18
Kingfisher 22
Macaw 18
Mandrill 10
Marshes 4
Moose 4
Mountains 6
North America 4, 16
Otter 16
Parrot 18
Platypus 20
Pond 4
Potto 12
Rivers 6
Russia 16
Seal 8
South America 6, 18
Tasmania 20

Glossary

Bill A bird's beak.
Filtering Taking out small objects from a liquid such as water.
Minute Very tiny.
Sensitive Something which is sensitive is good at feeling for things.
Webbed Having skin between the toes to help in swimming or paddling.